Al Jaffee
DRAWS A CROWD

by

Al Jaffee

D1559234

A SIGNET BOOK
NEW AMERICAN LIBRARY
TIMES MIRROR

Personally, I can't see what they think is so hilarious about this book.

NAL BOOKS ARE ALSO AVAILABLE AT DISCOUNTS IN BULK QUANTITY FOR INDUSTRIAL OR SALES-PROMOTIONAL USE. FOR DETAILS, WRITE TO PREMIUM MARKETING DIVISION, NEW AMERICAN LIBRARY, INC., 1301 AVENUE OF THE AMERICAS, NEW YORK, NEW YORK 10019.

© 1958, 1959, 1960, 1962, 1963, 1964, 1965, 1966
New York Herald Tribune, Inc.

Copyright © 1978 by Al Jaffee

All rights reserved

Ⓢ SIGNET TRADEMARK REG. U.S. PAT. OFF. AND FOREIGN COUNTRIES
REGISTERED TRADEMARK—MARCA REGISTRADA
HECHO EN CHICAGO, U.S.A.

SIGNET, SIGNET CLASSICS, MENTOR, PLUME and MERIDIAN BOOKS are published by The New American Library, Inc., 1301 Avenue of the Americas, New York, New York 10019

SIGNET, SIGNET CLASSICS, MENTOR, PLUME AND MERIDIAN BOOKS are published by The New American Library, Inc., 1301 Avenue of the Americas, New York, New York 10019

First Signet Printing, August, 1978

1 2 3 4 5 6 7 8 9

Printed in The United States of America

4 OUT OF 5 DOCTORS RECOMMEND

Al Jaffee DRAWS A CROWD

STOPS
BAD BREATH

CURES
HERNIA

PREVENTS
ATHLETE'S
FOOT

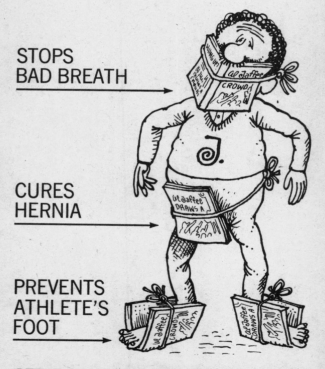

GET IT AT YOUR DRUGSTORE TODAY!
(Or wherever silly cure-alls are sold.)

Preface

Recently, in an earnest effort to find out why cartoons are funny, a nationally respected and highly esteemed polling organization interviewed 34,627,921 members of the rare and unusual profession of cartooning. The question they asked, one that is apparently uppermost in the minds of all non-cartoonists, was, "Where do you get your ideas?" A breakdown and analysis of their responses follows:

10,528,941 answered, "What ideas?"

8,926,436 answered, "From *The New York Times* obituary pages."

4,643,912 answered, "From interviews like this."

5,528,632 answered, "Get outta here, you clumsy ox! You knocked the ink bottle over on my work."

Later, back at the nationally respected and highly esteemed polling organization's headquarters, a large group of brilliantly trained and highly regarded specialists gathered to organize and analyze this important data.

Their report follows:

"Cartoonists are not as a group funny. This was clearly demonstrated by the answers they gave. Not a single cartoonist gave a funny answer or a funny source for his ideas. Thus, the inescapable conclusion has to be that cartoonists are *given* 'their' ideas."

That is to say, a cartoonist simply sits in his studio blankly staring at the wall until someone—be it wife, child, postman, etc.—walks in and says something like, "Hey, have I got a funny idea for you. See, there are these two guys taking their kids to the zoo. Suddenly, in the ape house, this big gorilla picks up a handful of garbage and flings it out at the people. The two guys and their kids get covered with the stuff and the crowd just absolutely breaks up laughing. Funniest thing I ever saw in my life."

This fantastically funny idea hits the cartoonist like a ton of bricks, and he instantly snaps out of his bleary-eyed lethargy and starts drawing. Soon a truly hilarious cartoon emerges and, of course, when it is printed in some nationally famous newspaper or magazine the public at large has a nice big laugh and everything.

"So," you may ask, "why don't cartoonists admit all this when they are asked where they get their ideas?" The answer to that, quite simply, is that it is physically impossible for a cartoonist to remember all the people who give him side-splittingly funny ideas. As we noted before, the ideas may come from a wife, child, postman, dentist, accountant, garbage man, plumber, barber and the thousands of other people he comes in contact with throughout his career.

Now that you, dear reader, know this, you are better prepared to read this book. But remember, if you find nothing funny in it, don't blame the cartoonist. After all, it was probably people not unlike yourself who inspired the ideas in it.

A flower story that smells to high heaven

9

(4)

⑤

MORE 11

(6)

Cartoon Folio Number One

I'll eat my hat before I'll read another page of this book.

14

15

16

17

18

A grapefruit section with a bitter taste

BVURCH!

Cartoon Folio Number Two

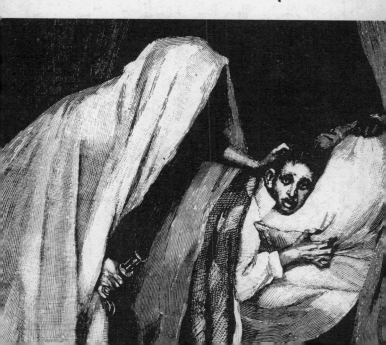

28

31

32

34

An automobile situation that runs out of gas

NO PARKING

2

36

NO PARKING

MORE

(4)

(6)

Cartoon Folio Number Three

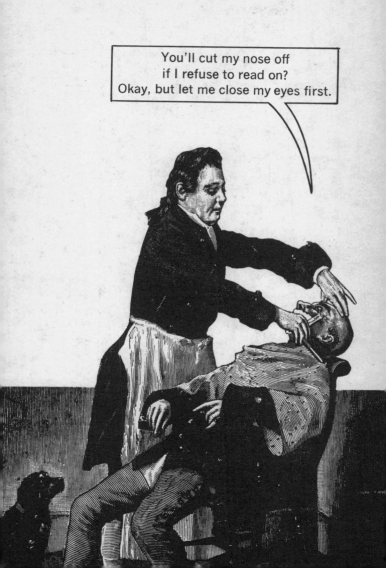

43

45

47

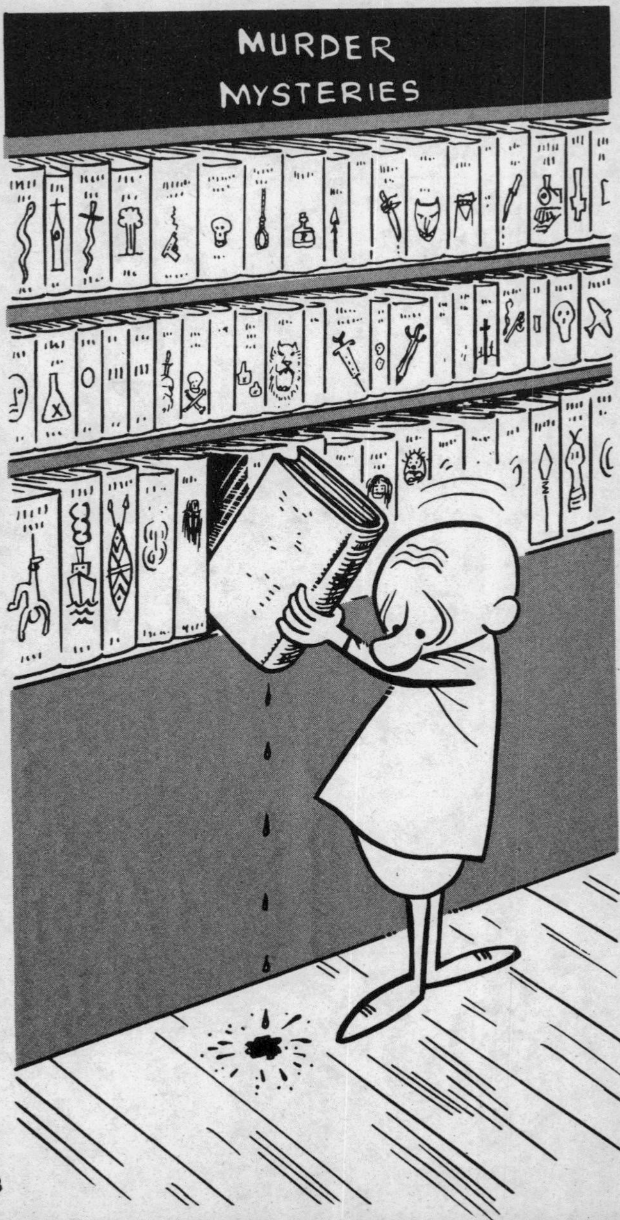
MURDER
MYSTERIES

A golfing experience that's certainly below par

MORE 53

Cartoon Folio Number Four

57

59

A helicopter thing that never gets off the ground

Cartoon Folio Number Five

67

68

69

A thing about a light bulb that'll turn everyone off

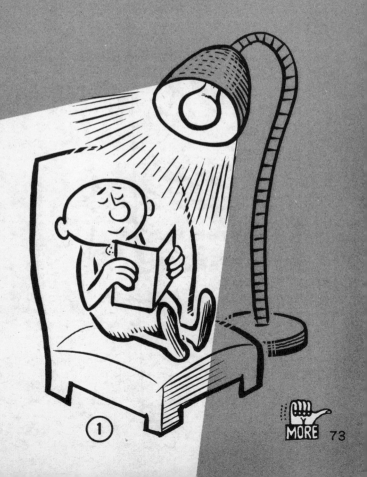

TINK!

MORE 77

(6)

Cartoon Folio Number Six

81

83

A tuba story
with a sour note

6

Cartoon Folio Number Seven

A breakfast tale that's somewhat tasteless

4

MORE 103

Cartoon Folio Number Eight

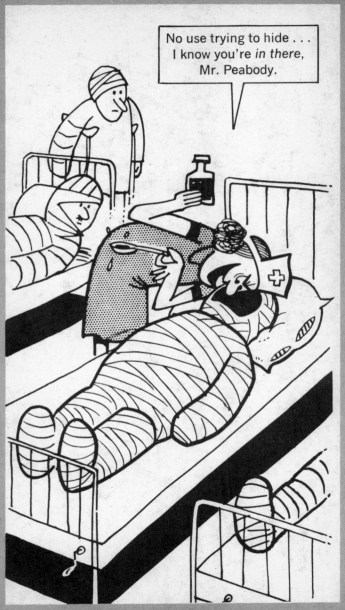

DO NOT
PICK
FLOWERS

110

A test of strength that's awfully weak

TEST
YOUR
STRENGTH

116

④

BONG

5

TEST
YOUR
STRENGTH

6

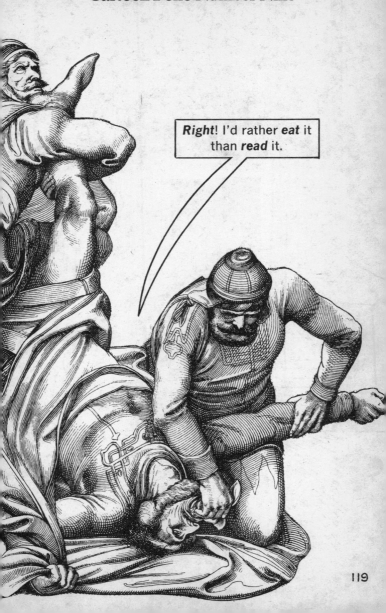

127

A funny-paper story that's nothing to laugh about

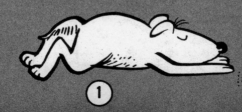

1

134

6

Cartoon Folio Number Ten

138

PROBLEMS
OF
ANIMAL
TRAINING

An equestrian story that horses around

MORE
143

②

MORE 145

4

6

152

154

FINE
IMPORTED WINES

155

156

A magic trick that isn't going to fool anybody

(1)

MORE 157

④

5

SILENCE STRICTLY ENFORCED

165

167

169

Another light-bulb story that isn't too bright

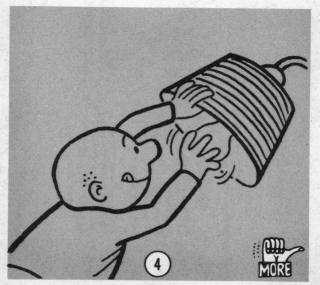

(5)

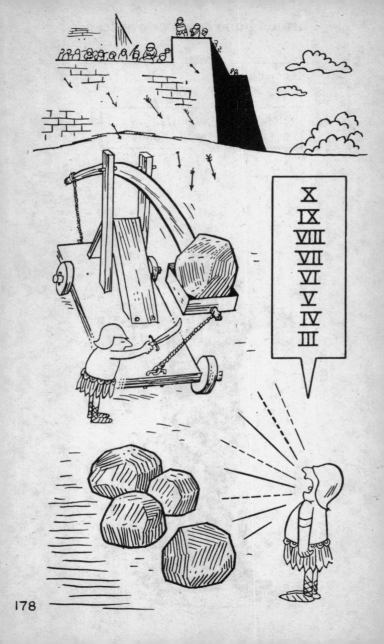

178

First guy said, "I'll take the check."
Second guy said, "No, let me."
First guy said, "I insist." Then . . .
CHECK

183

A hunting story that leaves you out in the cold

ZZZZZzzzz

191

HURRY, HURRY! BUY THESE BOOKS!

Only 12,256,67~~6~~ $4 copies of these treasured classics left in stock.

☐ **Al Jaffee Gags** . . . . (#Y6856—$1.25)

☐ **Al Jaffee Gags Again** . . . . . . (#Y6652—$1.25)

☐ **Al Jaffee Blows His Mind** . . . . . (#Y6759—$1.25)

☐ **Mad's Al Jaffee Spews Out MORE
   Snappy Answers to Stupid
      Questions** . . . . (#Y6740—$1.25)

☐ **The Mad Book of Magic
   by Al Jaffee** . . . . (#Y6743—$1.25)

☐ **Al Jaffee's Next Book** . . . . (#Y7625—$1.25)

☐ **Al Jaffee Illustrates
   Rotten Rhymes and
   Other Crimes by
   Nick Meglin** . . . . (#Y7891—$1.25)

☐ **Al Jaffee Bombs
   Again** . . . . (#Y7979—$1.25)

**THE NEW AMERICAN LIBRARY, INC.,
P.O. Box 999, Bergenfield, New Jersey 07621**

Please send me the SIGNET BOOKS I have checked above.
I am enclosing $_____(check or money order—
no currency or C.O.D.'s). Please include the list price plus
35¢ a copy to cover handling and mailing costs. (Prices
and numbers are subject to change without notice.)

Name_____

Address_____

City_____State_____Zip Code_____
Allow at least 4 weeks for delivery